THE 12 DISCIPLES OF JESUS

BOOK THREE

WRITTEN BY
TEMALESI W.M.K. SAVOU

ILLUSTRATED BY
BETHANY WHITWELL

ISBN: Softcover   978-1-5434-0325-1
        EBook   978-1-5434-0324-4

Print information available on the last page

Rev. date: 08/17/2017

To order additional copies of this book, contact:
Xlibris
1-800-455-039
www.xlibris.com.au
Orders@Xlibris.com.au

JAMES THE LESS

This is James. He is one of Jesus' disciples.

He is called 'James the Less".

James was born in Galilee, a city near the Sea of Galilee. It was ruled by the Roman government.

The apostle James is from Capernaum. It is a fishing village near the sea of Galilee.

CAPERNAUM

James lives with his father, Alphaeus and his mother Mary in Capernaum. He is also called James son of Alphaeus.

His mother is a relative of Mary the Mother of Jesus. She was the first person to see the empty tomb of Jesus.

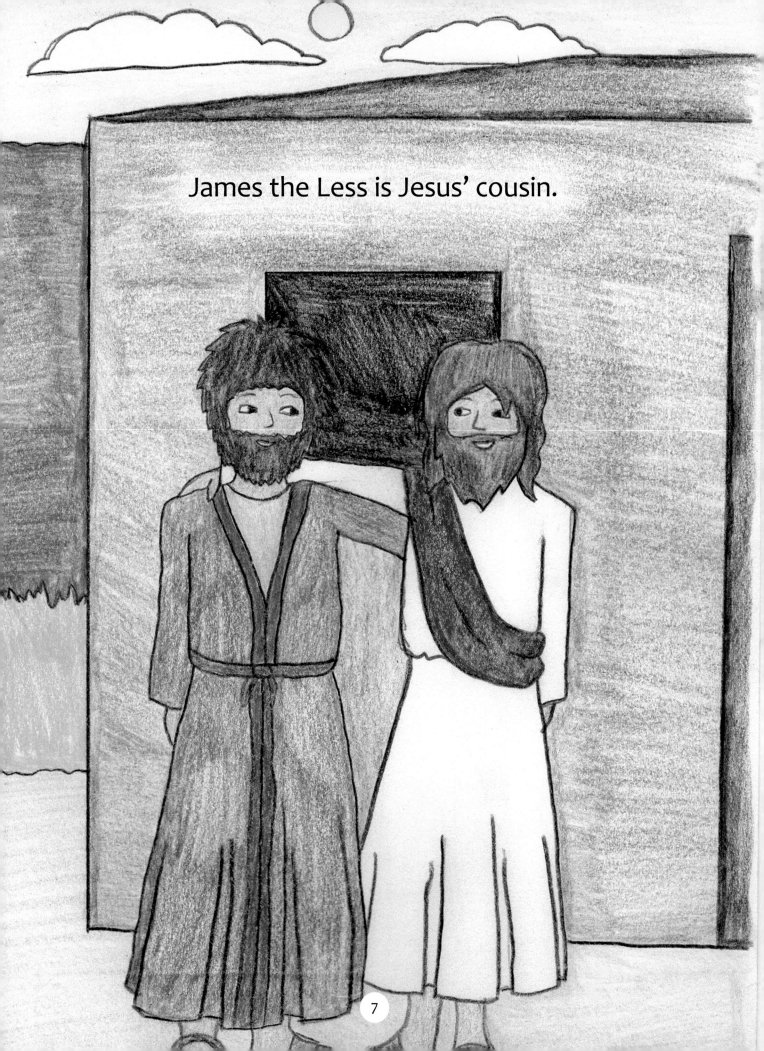

James the Less is Jesus' cousin.

James believed in Jesus, He believed that
Jesus is the son of the Almighty God.

James always enjoy telling people about all the miracles that Jesus had performed.

James even told the people how his mother,
Mary saw the empty tomb of Jesus.

James was a true friend of
Jesus, he loved Jesus.

JUDE

My Name is Jude some people call me Thaddaeus.

I am a Jew.

I was born in Galilee.

My father's name is Cleopas, some people called him Alphaeus and my mother's name is Mary.

My mother is the cousin of Mary
the mother of Jesus.

This is my brother. His name is James.

James and I were both chosen by Jesus to be his disciples.

I love to listen to Jesus' teachings.

I am always amazed to watch Jesus heal the sick people and give comfort to the poor.

I loved Jesus and would love to be like him.

SIMON THE ZEALOT

This is Simon. People called him Simon the Zealot.

Simon the Zealot was born in Judea.

Simon the Zealot lived with his
family in Capernaum.

Capernaum is a fishing village near the sea of Galilee.

Simon the Zealot is a businessman, he.
buys and sells a lot of things.

Simon the Zealot and Peter are very good friends.

One day, Peter visited Simon and told him about Jesus.

29

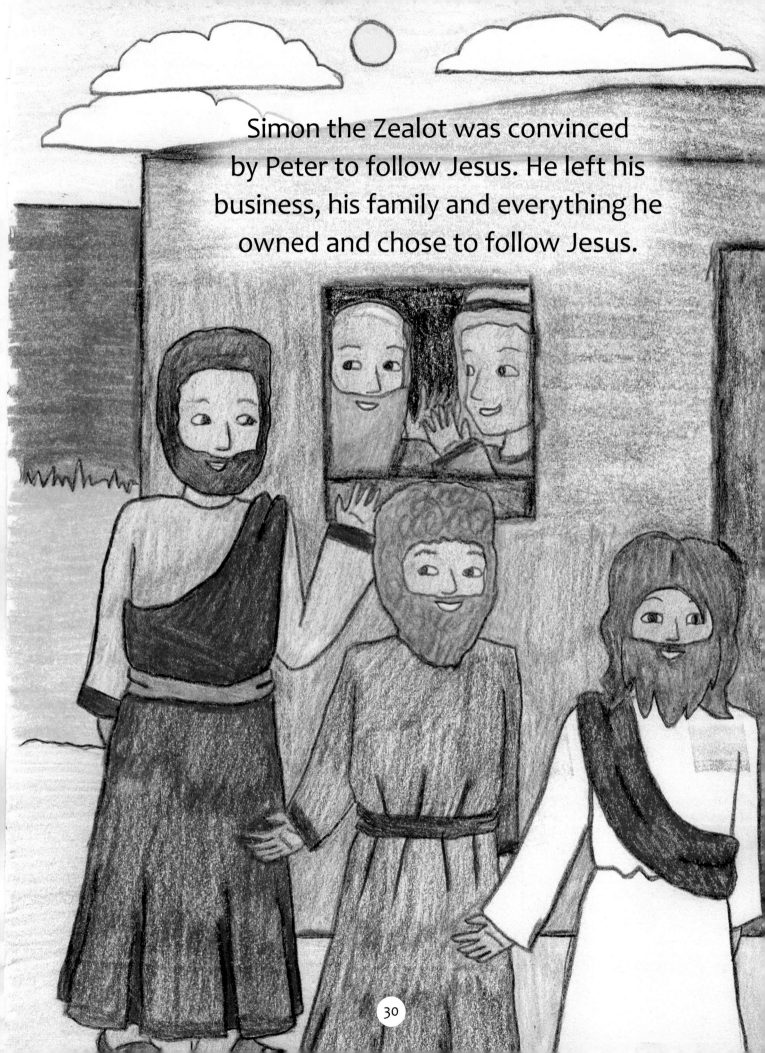

Simon the Zealot was convinced by Peter to follow Jesus. He left his business, his family and everything he owned and chose to follow Jesus.

Jesus loved Simon the Zealot and was always patient with him. They became very good friends.

JUDAS ISCARIOT

This is Judas Iscariot, He is one of the famous disciples of Jesus.

Judas Iscariot was born in a small town in Judea.

Judas Iscariot lived with his father,
Simon Iscariot in Jericho.

Judas Iscariot was an educated man, he learned a lot of things about running a business and also about the Kingdom of God.

Judas Iscariot was one of John the Baptist disciples. He loves to listen to John's preaching.

Judas Iscariot has a friend named Nathaniel.
Nathaniel is one of Jesus' disciples.

Nathaniel would share the story
about Jesus to Judas Iscariot.

One day, Nathaniel invited Judas Iscariot
to listen to the preaching of Jesus.

Jesus saw Judas Iscariot listening to his preaching, he called Judas and said, "follow me". Judas became Jesus' 12th disciples.

Printed in the United States
By Bookmasters